THE GREAT DANE PUPPY HANDBOOK

A Complete Guide to the First Year

Zach Reed

The Great Dane Puppy Handbook Copyright © Whistle Media LLC 2020

ALL RIGHTS RESERVED. This book contains material protected under International and Federal Copyright Laws and Treaties. Any unauthorized reprint or use of this material is strictly prohibited. No part of this book may be reproduced or transmitted in any form or by any means, electronic, mechanical, or otherwise, including photocopying or recording, or by any information storage or retrieval system without express written permission from the author.

Copyright and Trademarks. This publication is Copyright 2020 by Whistle Media LLC. All products, publications, software, and services mentioned and recommended in this publication are protected by trademarks. In such instance, all trademarks and copyright belonging to the respective owners. All rights reserved. No part of this book may be reproduced or transferred in any form or by any means, graphic, electronic, or mechanical, including but not limited to photocopying, recording, taping, scanning, or by any information storage retrieval system, without the written permission of the author. Pictures used in this book are royalty-free pictures purchased from stock photo websites with full rights for use within this work.

Published by Whistle Media LLC 2020

ISBN: 9781651864807

DISCLAIMER AND LEGAL NOTICE.

This product is not legal or medical advice and should not be interpreted in that manner. You need to do your own due diligence to determine if the content of this product is right for you. The author, publisher, distributors, and/or affiliates of this product are not liable for any damages or losses associated with the content in this product. While every attempt has been made to verify the information shared in this publication, neither the author, publisher, distributors, and/or affiliates assume any responsibility for errors, omissions, or contrary interpretation of the subject matter herein. Any perceived slights to any specific person(s) or organization(s) are purely unintentional. We have no control over the nature, content, and availability of the websites listed in this book. The inclusion of any website links does not necessarily imply a recommendation or endorse the views expressed within them. Whistle Media LLC takes no responsibility for, and will not be liable for, the websites being temporarily or being removed from the Internet. The accuracy and completeness of the information provided herein, and opinions stated herein are not guaranteed or warranted to produce any particular results, and the advice or strategies, contained herein may not be suitable for every individual. The author, publisher, distributors, and/or affiliates shall not be liable for any loss incurred as a consequence of the use and application, directly or indirectly of any information presented in this work. This publication is designed to provide information regarding the subject matter covered. The information covered in this book has been compiled to give an overview of the topics covered. The information contained in this book has been compiled to provide an overview of the subject. It is not intended as medical advice and should not be construed as such. For a firm diagnosis of any medical conditions, you should consult a doctor or veterinarian (as related to animal health). The writer, publisher, distributors, and/or affiliates of this work are not responsible for any damages or negative consequences following any of the treatments or methods highlighted in this book. Website links are for informational purposes only and should not be seen as a personal endorsement; the same applies to any products or services mentioned in this work. The reader should also be aware that although the web links included were correct at the time of writing they may become out of date in the future. Any pricing or currency exchange rate information was accurate at the time of writing but may become out of date in the future. The author, publisher, distributors, and/or affiliates assume no responsibility for pricing and currency exchange rates mentioned within this work.

Table of Contents

Chapter 1 Introduction 1

Chapter 2 Finding A Dog 3

    Breeder Considerations 4

    Shelter Considerations 7

Chapter 3 Preparing Your Home 9

    Establish The Puppy Zone 10

    Access To Food And Water 11

Chapter 4 Purchases To Consider 13

    Bedding 14

    Crate 14

    Great Dane Crate Criteria 15

    Toys 17

    Training Gear 18

Chapter 5 Feeding A Great Dane 20

    Food Types 21

    Food Recommendation 26

Sample Meal Plan 27

Meal Plan Recap 29

How to Change Foods 30

Raised Bowls 31

Chapter 6 Hygiene and Grooming 33

Nail Care 33

Ear Cleaning 36

Oral Care 39

Baby Teeth Transition 41

Brushing & Bathing 42

Chapter 7 Veterinary Care and Medical Decisions 45

Find A Veterinarian 45

First Visits 46

Vaccines 47

Flea, Tick, & Heartworm 50

Great Dane Heat 51

Spay and Neuter 54

Consider Pet Insurance 57

Chapter 8 Diarrhea Sources and Treatment 59

Dietary Indiscretion..60

Food Changes..60

Stress..61

Indigestible Substances..62

Parasites 62

Viral Infections..65

Bacterial Infection 66

Home Remedies for Diarrhea 66

When to See the Veterinarian About Diarrhea 68

Chapter 9 Additional Considerations 70

Exercise..70

Socialization..71

Puppy Biting...73

Pick A Training Approach 78

Potty Training 80

Registration Requirements..88

Chapter 10 Closing Thoughts..90

Chapter 1
Introduction

Congratulations! You've made the decision to bring a Great Dane into your life! As with many important life decisions, this is not one to be taken lightly. Caring for a Great Dane entails far more planning and diligence compared to that of smaller breeds. However, while there is an enormous amount of responsibility associated with caring for this giant breed, there is also a correspondingly wonderful amount of joy that they can bring to your life! By properly educating yourself in advance, you can avoid the pitfalls that plague many new owners.

The following chapters will detail the steps that a new owner should take to prepare for the arrival of a Great Dane puppy, as well as how to best care for them. For many of these steps, it is imperative that you take action on them prior to bringing your dog home. The phrase "proper planning prevents poor performance" is applicable now more than ever.

Keep in mind that while this guide is aimed at educating new Great Dane owners on how to care for a puppy, the majority of this information is also applicable to older Great Danes as well.

Chapter 2
Finding A Dog

While this may seem like a strange place to start, it's not uncommon for new Great Dane owners to spend years contemplating whether or not to bring a Great Dane into their family. Deciding where to get a dog will be one of your first big choices should you choose to make the leap.

While you may have already made this decision, understanding the considerations for working with a breeder or adopting from a shelter is still useful information. While there is no "right" answer, there are some considerations to account for in either case.

BREEDER CONSIDERATIONS

For many first-time Great Dane owners, working with a breeder will be the simpler option. Notice that I specifically used the word "simpler" in lieu of "better" because that is absolutely the case. Better requires a high degree of personal context that makes it impossible to generalize in this situation. Instead,

I will cover some of the advantages and disadvantages of working with a breeder to allow you to make your own informed decision.

ADVANTAGES TO WORKING WITH A BREEDER

Known Medical History: Perhaps the most valuable aspect of working directly with a Great Dane breeder is the ability to know the medical history of the dog's lineage. Good breeders will have spent a large amount of time locating the highest quality dogs for breeding. As such, these careful breeding selections can help to prevent expensive medical complications down the road.

On-Going Support: In addition to providing you with information immediately before and after purchase, many breeders welcome questions on an on-going basis as well.

Chapter 2 - Finding A Dog

They care deeply about the welfare of the puppies that they produce, and are often willing to assist or give advice in the event that issues do arise.

Personality Matching: Another valuable service that many breeders provide is to assist in matching you to an appropriate puppy. By best for you, I'm not referring to their external appearance but more so their personality. Training and working with an alpha male versus a more submissive personality will require different needs from the owner.

Selection Options: This item was intentionally saved for last, however, it is indeed a benefit of working with a breeder. If you have a preference for a male versus female or a particular color, you have far more choices when it comes to working with a breeder. If need be, you can even wait on a breeder's waiting list until a puppy meeting your specific requirements is produced.

DISADVANTAGES TO WORKING WITH A BREEDER

Higher Upfront Cost: One of the most apparent differences for working with a breeder will be the upfront cost. As a result of the care and due diligence that they put into breeding, top breeders often charge between $1,500 to $3,000 for a single puppy.

While these initial fees are higher, the total cost of ownership of the dog's lifetime is often lower by avoiding expensive medical care and procedures later in life.

Breeder Pre-Approval: While adoption clinics will spend some time assessing your ability to care and support a puppy, it likely will not be to the level that a breeder performs.

Many breeders require in-depth questionnaires to be completed as part of your assessment before being approved to join a waiting list. Because some people find this process invasive, it's worth noting as an expectation for working with a breeder.

Wait Times: Breeders do not always have puppies available. In fact, having to wait for availability is actually an indicator of a good breeder! They are not running puppy mills that constantly churn out puppies and often have waiting lists.

While waiting has a negative connotation in today's society, this should really be looked at as a positive. Waiting not only gives you time to prepare for a dog but also ensures that you're not making this big decision on a whim.

Chapter 2 - Finding A Dog

Shelter Considerations

Advantages to Working with a Shelter

Support A Good Cause: It can't be understated just how important it is to adopt dogs from shelters. Many shelters are underfunded and simply unable to support the large volume of animals sent to them. Not only will adopting from a shelter likely save a dog's life, but you'll be getting a dear friend for life.

Lower Upfront Cost: Compared to the fees of top breeders, adopting from a shelter typically costs in the neighborhood of $300 to $400. While this range will vary based on your geographical location and the age of the dog, it is far less than the initial cost of getting a puppy from a breeder.

Disadvantages to Working with a Shelter

Unknown Medical History: One key thing to keep in mind with adoption is that while the initial fees may be lower, that doesn't mean that the cost of caring for the dog over the course of their life will remain lower.

While it's certainly possible to find a purebred champion lineage Great Dane at the kennel, it's more likely that those who you come across were not bred under the best conditions. Unfortunately, these dogs may have not received the best veterinary care previously. There is no guarantee, but this may result in higher medical bills later in the animal's life.

This is not to say that an adopted Great Dane doesn't have a heart of gold - just that you need to be prepared for the potential of more health issues down the road.

Past History: Unfortunately, many dogs that you find in the shelter have not been treated well by their previous owners. From lack of training or socialization to cases of abuse, these are just a few of the areas that you may need to spend extra time working on with the dog after adoption. However, with time, patience, and love, your Great Dane will soon learn to trust and love you in return.

Limited Options: For most people adopting from a shelter, outward appearance is the least of their concerns. However, it's worth pointing out that you will have far less selection when it comes to age, gender, or coat color when adopting from a shelter.

Chapter 3
Preparing Your Home

One of the most important tasks before bringing home a Great Dane will be to dog-proof the house. While they may start out as "small" puppies, they will quickly grow into extremely large dogs that can reach virtually anything inside your home. If you are fortunate enough to bring them home as a puppy, it's important to teach them proper house manners before they are large enough to reach places that you didn't think were possible!

Setting your Great Dane up for success inside the home will be imperative. While accidents are inevitable, there are many things that you can do to help lessen their occurrence.

ESTABLISH THE PUPPY ZONE

While I deemed this the "puppy zone" it is better described simply as the "new dog zone." Regardless of whether you have an apartment or sprawling home, our human residences are far too big to allow your brand-new Great Dane to freely roam!

The more space they have to explore and inspect, the more likely that they will be to get into trouble. One of the best ways to limit this will be to establish a designated room or area for your new dog while they adapt.

Some common practical approaches to accomplishing this include:
- Assign an entire room
- Section off part of a room with a gate or divider
- Use a crate to limit access inside a larger room

Once you have created this area for your dog, take the time to remove any unnecessary clutter. Make sure to check areas both high and low as Great Danes will quickly have access to almost anything. This includes shelves, bookcases, end tables, etc… Tie up the drawstrings on blinds, elevate

Chapter 3 - Preparing Your Home

curtain bottoms, place laundry out of reach, and purchase lockable trash cans if they will be used in the space as well.

Remove absolutely anything that is not essential to the area. When in doubt - consider that each item left behind may be peed, pooped, drooled, or even chewed on by your new Great Dane. Take care to remove electrical cords as well as these are extremely dangerous if chewed on. Last but not least, keep in mind that fragile items may be accidentally damaged by your dog as well. From strong wagging tails to the zoomies, no item should be left unconsidered!

In addition to limiting the amount of trouble that they get in, the puppy zone is also helpful in allowing your Great Dane to adjust to their new surroundings. Coming to your home is a massive change for them, so keeping them primarily in one area will speed up this adjustment period. As they grow acclimated to your home, you can slowly increase their access.

ACCESS TO FOOD AND WATER

While the previous section primarily focused on what to remove or limit access to inside the puppy zone, two things that you should not restrict access to are food and water.

While you may choose to feed your Great Dane in a separate area of the house, they must absolutely have clean water available at all times.

Establish a plan for where bowls will be placed, and what steps you will take to limit potential messes. Great Danes are known for being messy drinkers, so you can expect a good amount of water drips and splashes around the bowl area. Many owners choose to place large plastic mats under the bowls as a way of catching the mess. Alternatively, if the room contains tiled sections then those areas should be considered prime locations for bowls.

Now that we've covered the basics of Dane-proofing your home, let's review some of the common purchases that you can expect to make when it comes to caring for a Great Dane.

Chapter 4
Purchases To Consider

Like it or not, purchasing a Great Dane is just the tip of the iceberg when it comes to caring for this giant breed dog.

I will review some of the most common purchase categories that you should plan to make for your dog, as well as considerations for selection.

Because the product recommendations themselves may change over time, I will instead cover key criteria to consider for each. In the event that you'd like to take a look at the products that I use for each category, all of them can be found at: https://greatdanecare.com/puppybook-products.

Bedding

Due to their large size and predisposition to a number of orthopedic issues, a high-quality bed is an extremely important investment for Great Danes. While typical beds work for average-sized dogs, they don't provide the necessary support for giant breeds like Great Danes. Beds that are specifically designed for larger breeds provide better support for their joints and help to relieve pressure points.

While good beds certainly cost money, there's no doubt that they will provide a good return on your investment. Danes are notoriously good sleepers, often sleeping 16-18 hours per day, and will be sure to put it to good use!

Crate

Although crate training remains a controversial topic, there is research to support the positive impact that they can have on your Great Dane. From an evolutionary standpoint, the desire to seek out enclosed spaces for safety is a deeply rooted instinct. Creating a space inside your home for your Dane to call their own helps satisfy this evolutionary desire.

In the absence of providing a place for them, you will inevitably find them curled up under a table or other enclosed

Chapter 4 - Purchases To Consider

space in an attempt to replicate a den. One key aspect that is often misunderstood is that crates are not for punishment. Your Dane should associate their crate as a place of comfort and safety, not where they are sent for a timeout.

By fostering their natural instinct and positive association to the crate i.e. den, your Dane will live a happier life. Separation anxiety is also less likely to be an issue when they feel safe and confident in their crates.

Crates are also a very helpful tool for potty training. Your Great Dane will want to keep their home clean and will hold it until taken to an appropriate place. Providing praise and rewarding them for these successful actions will further reinforce the positive behavior and have them potty trained before you know it. The topic of potty training will be covered in more detail in the training chapter of this book.

GREAT DANE CRATE CRITERIA

When it comes to a crate for your Great Dane, the saying "buy nice or buy twice" absolutely holds true. If you adopt them as a puppy they will weigh around 20 pounds.

forward to two years later as fully grown adults and they could weigh up to 200 pounds! This incredible change in size means that the size requirements for a crate will have also changed.

To avoid needing to buy a larger crate down the road, you should purchase one from the beginning that will also fit them as an adult. A high-quality crate that grows with your Dane rather than them growing out of is a wise choice.

The best crates come with movable sections that allow you to gradually increase the space for your Great Dane as they grow. This adjustability is what enables your Great Dane to use the same crate throughout their life.

A properly sized area is also important to the potty training process to reinforce their desire to not soil their home. Too much space allows them room to relieve themselves in one corner, and comfortably sleep in another.

While males are typically larger than females, the general recommendation is to go with a double extra-large crate regardless of the dog's gender. Common dimensions for these XXL crates are 45 inches tall, 35 inches wide, and 54 inches long. Crates should also be constructed of metal rather than plastic for durability.

Toys

One of the most common mistakes that new owners make is not having a variety of toys for their dog. Instead of assuming that your dog will prefer all hard chew toys like bones, make sure to include a selection of plush options as well. While soft toys may not last as long as hard ones, many Great Danes absolutely love them! They can be especially helpful for entertaining your Dane while they are going through teething phases.

Finding a good set of toys that your Great Dane enjoys not only makes life more enjoyable for them but is also a fantastic way to burn off excess energy through play. This is especially helpful for alleviating or preventing separation anxiety when they are left home alone. In addition to seeking out toys with added toughness, toys for Great Danes should also be physically larger to better suit them.

Training Gear

With a crate, bedding, and toys out of the way, another key area to consider will be the items related to training your Great Dane. While there are a wide variety of different training tools available, there are only a handful of truly critical items. Save yourself money by purchasing only the absolutely critical items in the beginning. You can always add more to your training kit over time as you realize the need for them.

1. **Collar**: A sturdy collar is important not just for training but also for affixing identification tags on your dog. Training-specific collars can certainly be considered later on, but for now, a basic one that allows you to attach a leash will suffice.
2. **Standard non-retractable leash**: Much like the collar, there are many options to pick from when it comes to your basic leash. However, the best option to go with will be a 6-foot non-retractable leash. These provide more control and strength compared to the retractable varieties, and as an added bonus are also cheaper! Do not spend the extra money on retractable leashes. They can teach bad habits and are not conducive to proper Great Dane training.

Chapter 4 - Purchases To Consider

3. **Long line leash**: In addition to your standard 6-foot non-retractable leash, investing in a long line leash is another very helpful tool for training. These allow you to work commands from a further distance, without the risk of having your dog dart away mid training. They range from 20 to 50 feet in length and are incredibly useful training tools.

Chapter 5
Feeding a Great Dane

Similar to crates, food is a hotly debated topic in the dog world! However, this is a worthy area for due diligence due to the impact that diet can have on a Great Dane's health. In addition to getting the appropriate nutrients, weight management is absolutely critical for this giant breed.

At this point in your journey, the key consideration should be to educate yourself on the feeding options available. Use this information to come to your own informed decision about which approach is best. Great Danes have sensitive digestive tracts and do not handle food switches well. Take the time to pick an approach that you feel comfortable adhering to for the long run, knowing that switches should be avoided if at all possible.

Chapter 5 - Feeding A Great Dane

FOOD TYPES

TYPE 1: KIBBLE

Kibble is the most common type of dog food found in the United States. It can be manufactured in large quantities and has a long shelf life, therefore making it one of the cheapest options available. Walking down the aisle of a grocery or pet store, you will likely see dozens of various kibble brands. This count can quickly balloon to hundreds of options when looking at online retailers such as Chewy.com.

Kibble is created by mixing together the ingredients and crushing them to create a dough-like compound. The "dough" is then fed into a pressurized machine where it's cooked and extruded into small bits of kibble.

Pros

- Cheap
- Good shelf life
- Easy to store
- Can be found in many locations
- Wide variety of brands and options to choose from
- Simple portion management
- Formulas available for different stages of life
- Easy to take on the go or travel with
- Simple cleanup after or around mealtime

Cons

- Its dry composition requires additional water intake to make up for lost fluids
- Product recalls are common due to contamination and other manufacturing mistakes
- Selecting one can be tough due to a large number of options
- Little regulation and oversight around food quality

Type 2: Canned

Canned food can almost be considered the wet equivalent of kibble. It's produced in mass quantities, and generally available in a variety of locations and brands.

Canned dog food is created by blending together raw and sometimes frozen meats. These are then ground into small bits, and then often supplemented with vitamins, minerals, or grains. This final mixture is then mixed and cooked before being canned. The cans are sterilized through a heating process before finally being shipped out for distribution.

Pros

- Increases the dog's water intake
- Good shelf life

- Can be found in many locations
- Soft consistency makes it easier to eat for dogs with oral issues
- Stronger smells may make it more appealing to dogs not wanting to eat i.e. elderly, sick, etc...

Cons

- More expensive than kibble
- Lower calorie density than kibble
- Can leave a mess to clean up
- Requires additional dental due diligence to prevent periodontal disease
- Needs to be used quickly or refrigerated after opening
- Not typically used as a standalone diet. Often combined with kibble or other supplementary food

Type 3: Semi-Moist

Interestingly, this type of dog food was popularized in the 1960s and 1970s and came in a hamburger-like patty. You may also see it referred to as "soft-moist" food. As the name entails, semi-moist acts as the happy middle ground to dry kibble and wet canned food. It contains more water than kibble but less than canned (usually in the 60% – 65% range).

Semi-moist foods do not require refrigeration and use preservatives to extend their shelf life.

Pros

- Easy to chew for dogs with oral issues
- More appetizing than dry kibble
- Less messy than canned food
- Cheaper than canned food

Cons

- More expensive than kibble
- High sugar and salt content can lead to loose stool for Great Danes
- Requires additional dental due diligence to prevent periodontal disease
- Many contain artificial flavorings and colorings

TYPE 4: RAW DIET (BARF)

The concept behind a raw diet is that your dog eats foods more closely aligned to their ancestral diet. In other words, they primarily eat meat, organs, and bones as the bulk of their diet. This often also includes a small portion of vegetables and fruits as well.

Contrary to what your own stomach may be telling you right now – this is not why it's also often called "BARF! It's

Chapter 5 - Feeding A Great Dane

an acronym that stands for "Biologically Appropriate Food" as well as "Bones and Raw Food."

To give you a better idea, a raw diet is typically composed of the following:
- 70% muscle meat
- 10% bone
- 5% liver
- 5% other secreting organs
- 10% fruits and vegetables

Pros

- Easier weight management
- Many owners report better musculature and healthier coats after switching to a raw diet
- Less poop to clean up
- Full control over your dog's diet

Cons

- Increased risk of exposure to harmful bacteria that could make you and your dog sick
- Requires more diligence to maintain a proper dietary balance
- Switching over may result in periods of diarrhea before the dog's body adjusts
- Typically more expensive

TYPE 5: HOME-COOKED

This option needs no introduction because it's what most of us do every day for our own food! Like a raw diet, you simply choose to take matters into your own hands and cook food for your dogs. A common example of this type of meal would be boiled chicken and rice or sweet potatoes. However, the options are virtually unlimited.

Pros

- Full control over your dog's food
- Cheaper than a raw diet
- Less chance of bacterial exposure due to cooking
- Cooking softens foods which can make them easier to consume for dogs with oral issues

Cons

- Requires more diligence to ensure proper dietary balance
- Additional time spent planning and prepping meals
- More expensive than kibble food
- May lead to more food stealing and begging

FOOD RECOMMENDATION

Given enough money, time, effort, and planning an owner can make any of these food options work. However, a high-

Chapter 5 - Feeding A Great Dane

quality kibble will be the best choice for the majority of owners to ensure that their Great Dane is consistently eating a balanced diet.

Balance is absolutely critical to ensuring proper development and has been found to be more difficult to execute than most owners assume. According to the Merk Veterinary Manual, a European study of home-prepared diets found that 60% of dogs had major nutrient imbalances. This just goes to show how tough it can be to ensure that you're providing your dog with a truly balanced diet.

Another advantage to kibble is that it is extremely easy to control the amount of food. Most foods will provide a set of feeding instructions that detail how much food to give your dog based on their weight. If your kibble does not provide these instructions, you can use the rough guidelines below for reference.

SAMPLE MEAL PLAN

The total food for a day should be evenly divided across each of the meals. Slowly increase the food throughout the month to match their increasing energy needs as they continue to grow. The number of meals that the food should be spread

The Great Dane Puppy Handbook

ss is also listed. Noticed how it transitions from 3 meals per day to 2 meals per day once they reach 5 months of age.

Age [months]	Food [cups]	Meals / Day
2	2 - 4	3
3	3 - 5	3
4	4 - 6	3
5	5 - 7	2
6	6 - 8	2
7	6 - 9	2
8	6 - 9	2
9	7 - 10	2
10	7 - 10	2
12 - 18 (female)	6 - 9	2
12 - 18 (male)	7 - 10	2

Females should start at the bottom of the range for a given month, and slowly have their food increased until reaching the low end of the following month. This should be a gradual increase that is spread evenly across the month's time frame. For example, a 3-month-old female would begin the month eating a total of 3 cups of food per day. Midway through the month, her daily food total would be at 3.5 cups. Finally, ending the month at 4 cups of food daily.

Chapter 5 - Feeding A Great Dane

Males should start in the middle of the range, and slowly have their food increased until reaching the middle of the range for the following month. As with females, this should be a gradual increase spread over the course of the month. As an example, a 5-month-old male would begin the month eating a total of 6 cups of food per day. Midway through the month, his daily food total would be at 6.5 cups. Finally, ending the month at 7 cups of food daily.

MEAL PLAN RECAP

Many Great Danes will not reach their full size and weight until three years of age. There should be no rush to bulk them up early or have the biggest pup in town. The goal should be to keep them light and lean until they reach the age of two.

Also, note that these are general guidelines for your Dane. If you notice them getting too lean then increase the amount of food. Lean is good, but restricting their calories too much will also negatively affect their development.

> For a quick visual indicator, you should be able to see their last rib when are standing when they are at the correct weight.

Likewise, if you're no longer able to see their last rib then they're probably past the "long and lean" stage. Hold off on increasing their food intake until they return to the proper body composition level.

As always - consult with your licensed veterinarian in the event that you are unsure or concerned about your Great Dane's health.

How to Change Foods

If you've done the proper homework upfront, then the need to change foods down the line will be dramatically lessened. However, there will still be some cases where your dog simply doesn't like the food, or you need to switch due to adverse reactions to it.

In the event that you decide to change your Great Dane puppy's food, you should not do so "cold turkey." An immediate change over between meals would be very tough on their stomachs leading to diarrhea, vomiting, or disruption of their growth pattern.

Chapter 5 - Feeding A Great Dane

Look to transition them fully from the old to food in three meals. You can further smooth the tran sprinkling a probiotic powder on top of the food before giving it to them.

- The first meal would be a mixture of 50% old food, 50% new food.
- Meal two would consist of 25% old food, 75% new food.
- Finally, the third meal would consist of 100% new food.

Raised Bowls

A classic hallmark of the Great Dane is their raised bowls. While shorter dogs can easily reach bowls placed on the floor, this becomes far less convenient for our tall Danes. For this reason, many owners choose to elevate their dog's food and water bowls. This is particularly helpful for reducing neck strain on older or aging dogs to ensure that they are easily able to reach their food and water.

You can establish the most suitable height simply by measuring your standing dog from the floor beneath their front paws up to the tops of their shoulders, then subtract approximately 6 inches. The bowl should be lined up directly with their lower chest. A typical full-grown Great Dane should have a bowl at a height ranging from 20 to 27 inches.

Another test is to see if your Dane is able to eat without stretching their necks upwards or having to lower or strain downwards. If their food seems to be in a comfortable position and they look happy, you've reached the perfect height!

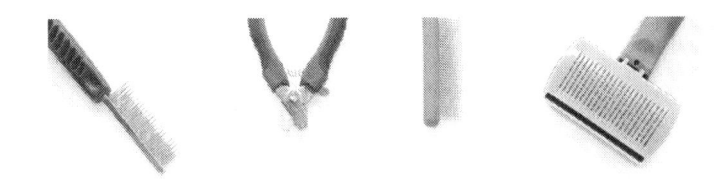

Chapter 6
Hygiene and Grooming

Compared to many other dogs, Great Danes are a relatively low maintenance breed. While there is not a long list of steps related to hygiene and grooming, these are not items that you want to let fall by the wayside.

Nail Care

While it can be easy to overlook, nail care is essential for your Great Dane. As a larger, heavier breed, your Great Dane's paws take on more work than smaller breeds. Nail maintenance that is neglected for extended periods can result in deformed feet and damaged tendons.

Like many breeds, not all Great Danes are comfortable with getting their nails trimmed. Some who particularly despise the process may even get aggressive when it's time for their regular nail trim. As a result, some dog owners make the decision to use professionals for their grooming needs. The good news for you is that nail maintenance is actually a very straightforward process that you can perform at home.

One of the best ways to get your Great Dane comfortable with nail maintenance is to first get them accustomed to having their paws handled. From the earliest possible time, you should practice holding their paws and evening massaging their pads or toes to get used to the sensation. This will allow them to be much more relaxed during the trimming process.

WHEN TO CUT A GREAT DANE'S NAILS

The amount of time in-between trims will vary most based on the type of surface that they typically walk on. For example, if your dog spends much of their day walking on the soft carpet, their nails will experience far less natural wear compared to walking on a hard surface such as concrete. The more natural wear that occurs, the less often you will need to trim their nails. Note that diet and genetics can also play a factor in the speed of nail growth.

However, the general rule is if your dog is standing up and his or her nails are hitting the floor, then they are ready for a trim. To get their dog accustomed to the process, many owners simply trim their dog's nails once every 1-2 weeks. While their nails may only have grown a small amount, this regular practice allows both you and the dog to get used to nail trimming.

How to Cut a Great Dane's Nails

I recommend using either a scissor style clipper or nail grinder for trimming your Great Dane's nails. The scissor-style is particularly useful for its enhanced cutting power and ability to fit around the larger nails of Great Danes. For owners not comfortable with the scissor style, nail grinders will be a good alternative. While there is less risk of hitting your dog's quick with grinders, some Great Danes do not like grinders because of their noise or vibration.

Using either a grinder or clipper, slowly trim back the nail at a 45-degree angle to follow the slant of the nail growth (see image on next for reference). The nail and the quick grow at roughly the same angle, and if you stick to that you can trim the nail shorter while avoiding the quick. Use multiple small cuts to take back the nail in small increments.

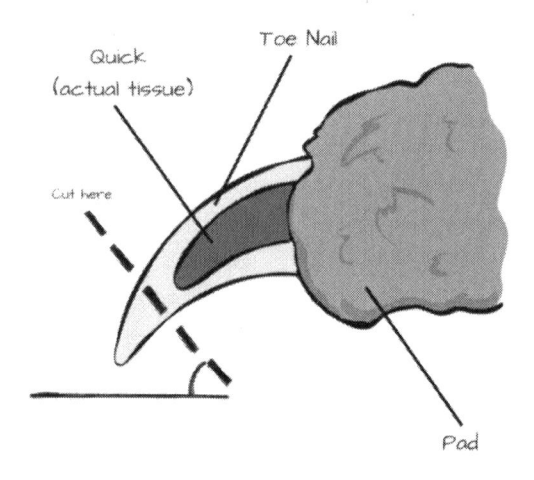

Toe Nail
Quick (actual tissue)
Cut here
Pad

Do NOT attempt to make large cuts. This will inevitably result in hitting the quick and causing your dog pain and bleeding. If you do accidentally cut into your dog's quick, make sure to have styptic powder on hand to stop the bleeding.

EAR CLEANING

As you will soon find out, Great Dane's ears can get dirty very quickly! Regardless of what you have heard, your Dane's ears will pick up a surprising amount of gunk whether they have been cropped or left natural. It is important to

Chapter 6 - Hygiene and Grooming

clean them on a regular basis to prevent infections from occurring.

In the event you notice your Dane intently scratching at their ears, then it's a good sign that you're overdue for a cleaning session. Another common sign that your Great Dane needs their ears cleaned is when they shake their heads aggressively in an attempt to "scratch the itch". You can also tell that they're ready for an ear cleaning by simply looking inside their ears. If you can see wax or dirt in their ear, then that's a sure sign that it's time to clean them!

You should plan to develop a consistent routine based on your veterinarian's recommendation, however, cleaning their ears once per week is a common starting point.

How to Clean a Great Dane's Ears

While ear wipes allow you to clean the upper parts of the ear, they will never be able to reach the deeper parts of your dog's ear. For this reason, it's important to use an ear cleaning solution to help flush debris from the deepest parts of the ear canal. Once it has been loosened and flushed out, you can easily remove it using cotton balls or ear wipes.

1. Gently lift the dog's ear back and slightly up and squeeze a liberal amount of cleaning solution into the ear canal. Fill the ear canal until you are able to see a visible fluid line.
2. While still holding the ear, gently massage the base of the ear in a circular motion to help loosen any debris that is deep inside of the ear. You should be able to hear an audible sucking or squishing sound while massaging the base of their ear.
3. Continue to massage the ear for at least 30 seconds to allow the cleaning solution to loosen the debris. *Note:* you may need to hold your dog's muzzle to prevent them from tipping their heads to dump out the fluid.
4. Once this is complete, allow your Great Dane to vigorously shake their head. This not only removes the liquid but will also help to shake out any of the accumulated debris. *Note:* It can be helpful to have a large towel present to place around their heads while they are shaking it to prevent making a mess. Alternatively, you can perform the cleaning in a room that you do not mind getting a little dirty, or even consider going outside.
5. Use a cotton ball or ear wipe to remove any visible debris. Do not dig deep into their ear, just focus on wiping the areas that your hand can reach.

Chapter 6 - Hygiene and Grooming

6. Continue using a cotton ball or ear wipe to trace around the finer outer ridges of the ear as debris often accumulates in these areas as well.
7. If the ear is particularly dirty, you may need to repeat these steps 1-6 again for the same ear.
8. Repeat this process for the opposite ear once the first is clean.

ORAL CARE

According to the American Veterinary Medical Association, 80 percent of dogs show signs of oral disease by age 3. Not only can gum disease result in tooth loss and bad breath, but it can even affect your dog's organs. Bad bacteria from diseased teeth and gums can migrate to your dog's kidneys, liver, heart, and even their joints. By spending just a few minutes a day taking care of your dog's teeth and gums, you can help protect them from dental diseases and all of the health issues that they can cause.

A dog-specific toothbrush and toothpaste are the most common approach. However, there are also fantastic sprays, gels, wipes, and enzymatic cleaning solutions available for use. The non-brush options are particularly useful for Great Danes who are finicky about you poking around in their mouth. Like other types of grooming, you can help to prevent this issue from occurring by introducing them to dental hygiene at an early age.

Figure out which approach to dental care works best for you and your dog, then be sure to practice it every day. Plaque and tartar build-up faster than you might think, so it is important to stay committed to your dog's dental cleanings.

You can also combine or rotate multiple teeth cleaning methods to ensure consistency if needed. Keep wipes or sprays on hand for busy days when you don't have time for a good brushing. Alternatively, give your dog a dental chew daily and just perform brushing on the weekends when you have more time. Multiple options will help ensure that your dog's teeth are taken care of, even on the most hectic days.

How to Brush a Great Dane's Teeth

Brushing your dog's teeth is very similar to brushing your own teeth. This is something that you will want to introduce to them at an early age. In the beginning, you may even want to start by rubbing a small amount of toothpaste on their teeth and gums to get them used to the sensation. Reward or praise the dog to help them form a positive association with

Chapter 6 - Hygiene and Grooming

teeth cleanings. Slowly work up to a full brushing session, continuing with the rewards and praise, as your dog becomes more comfortable with the experience.

1. Before starting, make sure to pick up a dog-specific toothbrush and toothpaste. Long-handled toothbrushes are particularly helpful for reaching the deeper parts of their large mouths.
2. Apply toothpaste to the toothbrush and brush gently, in a circular motion. Make sure to brush each tooth completely.
3. You should brush your dog's gums as well but do so lightly. You just want to stimulate the gums to clean them and improve circulation.

BABY TEETH TRANSITION

Your Great Dane will start their life with around 28 baby teeth. Over time these will fall out and be slowly replaced by 42 permanent adult teeth. This process will usually begin when your dog is about three months old, though some dogs start a little later. In most cases, these baby teeth will come out all on their own. Eating, chewing, and playing takes care of them in most cases.

However, sometimes a permanent tooth will start to emerge before the baby tooth has fallen out. It is important to examine your dog's teeth often during this transition period and keep an eye out for irregularities like this. The permanent tooth may force the baby tooth out on its own in a few days. If it does not, or if your dog seems to be uncomfortable or in pain, a trip to the vet may be in order. They can extract the stubborn baby tooth, allowing the permanent tooth to come in normally.

Also, it's important to note that not every Great Dane will develop all 42 adult teeth. Some may have a few less, and as long as they only have a couple missing there shouldn't be a cause for concern. However, you should be careful when brushing around areas with missing teeth. These spots may be more sensitive or easily damaged, so be extra gentle when brushing around these areas.

Brushing & Bathing

Baths

Thanks to their short hair, Great Danes have very low bathing needs compared to breeds with long hair. Bathe them only as needed, if they smell, or are dirty. One common mistake that many new Great Dane owners make is to bathe

Chapter 6 - Hygiene and Grooming

their dog too often! Doing so can result in dry and flaky skin, and will also reduce the sheen of their coats. For many Great Danes, bathing them once every 1-3 months will suffice. While not its main purpose, bathing can also help to remove dead hair to reduce shedding.

Stick to gentle, dog-friendly shampoos to help prevent their skin from being unnecessarily dried out. Also, make sure to avoid using human shampoos as they may be too harsh and upset the pH balance of their skin.

As has been repeated for many other Great Dane related grooming tasks, bathes are something that you will introduce to your dog at an early age. They will be much harder to coerce into the water as they grow, so get them as comfortable as possible with the process from a young age. Because Great Danes get cold easily, make sure to use warm water for baths. Freezing cold or burning hot water will only increase their dislike of the process.

BRUSHING

While brushing a Great Dane is not a required grooming task, it's more useful than most owners realize! For starters, brushing is the most effective way to remove dead hairs from a Great Dane's coat and reduce the shedding around your home. This is why spending 5-10 minutes brushing your dog between baths is so effective.

Brush their coats once per week, and you should find a drastic reduction in the amount of shedding. Hold the brush roughly parallel to their body, and make long gently sweeping strokes. Start from near their head, and slowly work your way down their body. Avoid using too much pressure as it can irritate their skin. Brushes with soft rubber tips are preferred to those with metal or wire tips to avoid digging into their skin.

In addition to removing dead hair, brushing also helps to spread around the natural oils found in a Great Dane's coat and enhance its sheen and appearance.

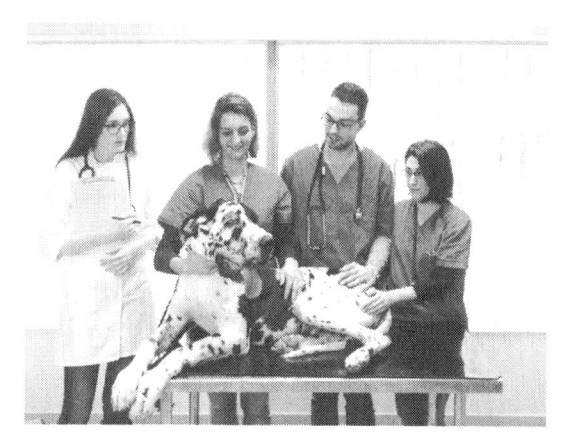

Chapter 7
Veterinary Care and Medical Decisions

Find a Veterinarian

Like many other giant breeds, Great Danes are predisposed to a number of elevated health risks. Hip dysplasia, bloat, or Wobblers syndrome are just a few of the ailments that could affect them, making the need for good health care that much more important.

Before bringing your Great Dane home you should have already met with and selected the veterinarian that will be providing long term care for your dog. If you have the luxury of several vets in your local area, meet with all of them to see who you think will be the best fit.

Some evaluation criteria that you may want to consider when meeting with different vets include:

- Past experience working with Great Danes
- Friendliness of staff
- Cleanliness of facilities
- Distance from your home or work
- Convenient hours of operation (days and times)
- After-hours emergency care availability
- Costs (estimates for common care, option to split payments or use a line of credit if needed)

FIRST VISITS

In addition to identifying and selecting a veterinarian, you should expect to make many visits to see the veterinarian over the course of your puppy's first year of life. Also, plan to take your dog for their first visit within 1-3 days of coming home. Not only is this required by most breeders, but doing so will ensure that your new puppy has a clean bill of health.

- A first appointment will typically include:
- Official weigh-in
- Listening to the heart and lungs
- Inspection of their eyes, ears, nose, mouth, teeth, feet, and genitalia
- Stool sample analysis

Chapter 7 - Veterinary Care and Medical Decisions

Additionally, first visits also often involve a conversation with your veterinarian regarding whether or not you plan to microchip your Great Dane. This involves implanting a small microchip, about the size of a grain of rice, under your dog's skin. The process is quick and relatively painless to your dog but allows for quick and easy identification in the event that they are lost. While there is a small fee associated with microchipping, it's nominal in the grand scheme of things and is one of the best ways for identifying lost pets. However, it's important to note that microchips only contain pet identification numbers, and do not provide GPS tracking capabilities.

VACCINES

In addition to a physical exam, your veterinarian will also want to ensure that your new puppy is up to date on their vaccines. Vaccines prevent illnesses by introducing a small dose of the disease to the immune system and allowing for the creation of antibodies to fight it off without infecting the dog. Vaccines are incredibly important to ensuring your Great Dane's long term health and are not to be taken lightly.

Additionally, if you wish to utilize a doggy daycare or boarding service at some point, these businesses will require proof of up-to-date vaccination records before allowing your dog into their facilities.

Below is an outline of the generally accepted puppy vaccination schedule for the core vaccines. Core vaccines include prevention for parvovirus, distemper, hepatitis, and rabies.

Non-core vaccines are given depending on the dog's exposure risk. These include vaccines against Bordetella bronchiseptica, Borrelia burgdorferi, and Leptospira bacteria. As always, follow your veterinarian's recommendation for any non-core vaccines.

Age	Vaccine
6 – 8 weeks	Distemper and parainfluenza
10 – 12 weeks	DHPP
12 – 24 weeks	Rabies
14 – 16 weeks	DHPP
12 – 16 months	Rabies, DHPP
Every 1 – 2 years	DHPP
Every 1 – 3 years	Rabies (as required by local law)

Note: DHPP refers to a combination of distemper, adenovirus (hepatitis), parainfluenza, and parvovirus.

Chapter 7 - Veterinary Care and Medical Decisions

Although vaccines are highly recommended and are generally safe for dogs, it is important to realize that they do not come without risk. According to the American Animal Hospital Association "In general, all canine vaccines are quite safe and only a small percentage of vaccinated dogs, regardless of the type of vaccine, develop severe adverse reactions."

You should be aware of the various reactions before heading to the vet so you can be prepared to act if your puppy begins to act strangely or exhibit any symptoms. Note that your dog will likely be tired or sleepy after a vaccine, so that is not considered an adverse reaction. Most dogs will also experience some amount of soreness at the injection site afterward, but it should not limit their activity.

Although rare, allergic reactions to vaccines do happen. If your Great Dane presents any of the severe symptoms listed below after a vaccination, take them to a vet or animal hospital immediately:

- Facial swelling
- Hives
- Difficulty breathing
- Collapsing
- Seizures

If your puppy seems stable but is experiencing any of the less severe symptoms listed below, call your vet for further instructions:

- Fever over 103 degrees
- Loss of appetite for more than a few days
- Repeated vomiting
- Continuous diarrhea
- Severe swelling, redness, or pain at the injection site

FLEA, TICK, & HEARTWORM

In addition to vaccines, your veterinarian will also likely make recommendations for flea, tick, and heartworm prevention. While flea and tick may be optional depending on where you live and the activities that you plan on doing with your dog, heartworm prevention should be taken very seriously.

Heartworm disease is one of the most well-known pet diseases, and it is estimated by the American Heartworm Society that over one million dogs in the US are affected. It is easy to prevent, but once infected, it can be very difficult to get rid of and can even be fatal. This is why veterinarian's include a heartworm blood test as part of your dog's annual checkup.

Chapter 7 - Veterinary Care and Medical Decisions

While there are medical and surgical approaches to treating heartworms, they can be expensive and extremely taxing on your dog. For these reasons, prevention is by far your best solution to heartworms.

As you can see, from vaccinations to flea and tick treatments, there will be many scheduled (and probably unscheduled) visits to the veterinarian in the first year of your Great Dane's life.

GREAT DANE HEAT

Most breeds reach sexual maturity and experience their first heat at around six months of age. However, Great Danes may not experience their first heat until they are two years old. That being said, every dog is unique, and some may have their first heat much sooner.

Because the timing of a first heat's arrival can vary, it's important to understand the signs that your dog may be in heat. Common indicators that your Great Dane is in heat include:

- **Bleeding or licking:** The most obvious sign that your Great Dane is going into heat is vaginal bleeding.

However, before she begins bleeding, you may notice some redness and swelling in her genital area. During this time, many Great Danes lick their vulva more than usual as well.

- **Increased urination:** Increased urination is another sign of the onset of heat. Her urine at this time contains high levels of pheromones and hormones, so she may begin marking more often. This is her way of letting nearby males know that she will soon be fertile. Males can smell these markings from miles away, so you may begin to see more male dogs coming around your home.

- **Personality changes:** The changes in hormone levels may result in temporary personality changes as well. If your dog is normally more independent or aloof, you may notice that she wants more attention than usual. She may also have less patience for other dogs and become a bit snippy. While this type of behavior certainly should not be encouraged, refrain from over correcting her knowing that the behavior is related to her hormonal state. Keep in mind that this behavior is only temporary, and you don't want to make her feel unsupported by her human family.

- **Nesting behaviors:** Many dogs also display nesting behaviors and begin preparing a place for their pup-

Chapter 7 - Veterinary Care and Medical Decisions

pies. Some may even show increased attachment to toys and stuffed animals, caring for them as if they are puppies. This usually occurs during the diestrus phase, after ovulation.

Heats typically last three weeks, so you will need to remain vigilant to ensure that your dog does not become pregnant during this time. Her body will produce pheromones and hormones that males dogs can smell from up to three miles away. A determined Great Dane will be tough to stop, so you need to prepare an escape-proof area before your dog's heat cycle begins.

It is best to limit the amount of time your dog is outside while she is in heat, and you should never leave her outside alone. It is absolutely essential that you keep her away from intact males in order to prevent pregnancy. You should also be cautious about walking her on a leash in open areas. Male dogs can and will attempt to mate with her even while she is on a leash. She may also attempt to run or break free of her leash if she senses a potential mate in the area. It is best to keep her in confined areas if at all possible, even while leashed.

Some dogs bleed very little and are able to keep themselves clean, but many have a heavier flow that can create a mess. Dog diapers are the perfect solution for keeping blood off of your floors, walls, and furniture. Your dog may already be a bit grumpy while she is in heat, so it's best to teach her to wear one early. Get her used to wearing it and comfortable with it before her first cycle begins.

While disposable diapers might be tempting, it can be difficult to find ones that are both large and flexible enough to fit a Great Dane. Washable female dog cloth diapers provide a much better fit, and even have pre-cut holes for their tails! They also have stretchy elastic straps that let you cinch it up just right so that your Dane is still able to comfortably move around.

Spay and Neuter

With the exception of experienced breeders, most owners will choose to have their Great Dane spayed or neutered. General advice on this topic can be confusing because smaller breeds often have these procedures performed as early as only a few months in age. However, research and anecdotal evidence indicate that spaying or neutering Great Danes too soon is detrimental to their long-term health.

Chapter 7 - Veterinary Care and Medical Decisions

Great Danes grow at an incredible rate in the first year of life. By postponing this procedure you give their bodies the necessary time to develop. This includes both physical and hormonal development; the latter of which being especially important.

For males, this means that neutering should not be conducted until they are at least one year of age. This ensures that they have a chance to fully develop the musculature needed to support their massive frames. Many Great Danes who are neutered too young have the appearance of a gangly puppy for their entire life.

The age for spaying females is similar, however, the timing around their estrus period needs to be considered. This consists of approximately 3 weeks during which they are "in heat" as well as the following two months. The risk of clots is much higher due to their elevated hormones and could result in death.

Because the timing of the first heat can vary, a spay is often performed following the female's first estrus period. In the event that their first heat does arrive early, you should still wait until they are at least one year old before spaying.

Most dogs (male and female) go home the same day that these surgeries are performed once they have recovered from the anesthesia. However, some clinics may require them to stay overnight for further monitoring. Once they return home it typically takes 18-24 hours for the anesthesia to fully clear their system.

During this time, it's very likely that they will be groggy and sleepy. It is best to keep them in a quiet area away from other pets or children while they recover. You may also notice that they may also eat less than normal due to nausea symptoms from the anesthesia.

While they may want to resume normal activity after a few days, you will need to restrict their physical activity for two weeks after surgery. This will allow the surgical incisions to fully heal, and reduce the chance of complications. Avoid bathing your Great Dane during this time as it could increase the risk of infection.

You should also make use of an Elizabethan collar through the entirety of the healing process. This large cone will prevent them from licking or biting at the surgical site that can get itchy during healing. Finally, you should inspect the surgical site twice a day to check for any negative changes or signs of infection. The most common signs of infection include unusual pus or discharge, a foul odor, inflammation, or the incision area being hot to the touch.

CONSIDER PET INSURANCE

Like it or not, giant breeds can come with giant medical bills when things go wrong. From accidents and illnesses to hereditary diseases, the costs can quickly add up. Much like human health insurance, pet insurance is there to help cover the cost of veterinary care when these unfortunate events do occur.

To get a better understanding of some of these health risks lets review a few of the most common health issues for Great Danes. Next to each condition, we've listed its average cost of diagnosis and treatment.

Some common health issues affecting Great Danes include:
- Bloat (GDV): $1,500 – $7,500
- Hip Dysplasia: $1,500 – $6,000
- Osteochondrosis of the shoulder: $2,000 – $4,000
- Entropion: $500 – $1,500
- Cardiomyopathy: $500 – $1,500

Note: This data is based upon actual claims paid out by Embrace Pet Insurance.

As you can see from just a few sample health conditions, the cost of care can quickly become overwhelming. While paying these bills 100% out of pocket will always be an option, pet insurance can go a long way in bringing peace of mind. For a fraction of the cost of care, you'll always be able to afford veterinary care if needed.

One common mistake that I see being made is thinking of pet insurance as being similar to home or auto insurance. While those options will be rarely or possibly never needed, it's almost guaranteed that your Great Dane will be injured or ill at some point in their lifetime.

While this is certainly not a topic that anyone will enjoy discussing, pet euthanasia is a very real thing. These "economic euthanasia" situations occur when a pet owner is unable to afford the care for their animal, and rather than let them continue to live in pain the veterinarian is forced to put them down. Regardless of how you feel about the morality of this situation, it's one that no pet owner ever wants to experience or even have to consider for that matter.

Whether or not you choose to purchase pet insurance, it's incredibly important to have a plan in place to understand exactly how you might pay for these bills if the situation does arise.

Chapter 8
Diarrhea Sources and Treatment

While diarrhea certainly falls into the medical category, it is unfortunately common enough amongst Great Dane puppies that it deserves an entire chapter. Great Danes have sensitive stomachs and digestive tract, making them more susceptible to diarrhea.

Many puppies experience soft stool until they are one year old, and will likely encounter diarrhea several times before adulthood. Luckily, many of these cases are due to harmless sources. If it persists, seek veterinary assistance as it could be a sign of something more serious.

The most common sources of Great Dane puppy diarrhea are described below.

Dietary Indiscretion

If your Great Dane puppy has diarrhea, one possible source is a dietary indiscretion, or a circumstance also known as "garbage gut". This is when the dog eats too much or eats something that its body cannot break down. This can either be garbage, table scraps of human food, grass, or anything foreign to a normal canine diet.

Common signs that your pup has experienced a dietary indiscretion include:
- Diarrhea
- Vomiting
- Lack of appetite
- Weakness

This condition is very similar to what humans experience when they get food poisoning. These episodes are typically short-lived and clear up within 24-72 hours.

Food Changes

Owning a Great Dane comes with the territory of caring for their sensitive stomachs. If your Great Dane has recently

Chapter 8 - Diarrhea Sources and Treatment

been introduced to different food, it is possible they will develop diarrhea. If you are thinking about making the switch to a new brand of food – take it slow! Your canine buddy will thank you! Great Danes need time for their touchy bellies to process and adjust to changes. One way to wean him away from his previous diet is to mix in the new food very gradually. Refer back to the feeding section regarding guidelines for switching foods.

STRESS

Dogs can undergo stress for a variety of reasons. Has anything in your Great Dane's life changed recently? Certain life events, whether in your or their life, can upset the stomach and trigger incidents of diarrhea. These big dogs are very sensitive to things that are happening in their environment.

Have you moved, had a baby, put them in a kennel, been around new people, or changed your work schedule lately? All these changes could have an effect on your pet and disrupt their sensitive digestive system.

For instance, when puppies are brought into a new home, it is normal for them to be nervous and excrete soft stool. The abdominal distress can last up to a couple of days, but it's nothing to worry too much about. Once puppies get adjusted to their new family, food, and schedule, the symptoms will subside and they will be back to their usual cheery selves.

While dietary indiscretion, food changes, and stress are the most common reasons for Great Dane puppy diarrhea, they are far from the only ones. Listed below are some of the additional sources.

INDIGESTIBLE SUBSTANCES

Puppies are naturally playful and rambunctious. Great Danes love exploring new houses and yards. If you aren't watchful, they could get into things they are not supposed to. Potential hazards like toys, socks, rock, and other small objects are easy targets for your curious pet to go after. These can cause blockage in their intestines and make them sick.

If you suspect your puppy has eaten a foreign object, take them to the vet to get examined. They may perform scans to locate the object, but in most cases wait for it to pass.

PARASITES

Great Danes and other dogs alike are susceptible to assorted parasites. The most common ones live in the gut. They are

Chapter 8 - Diarrhea Sources and Treatment

contracted either by coming in contact with mammal carriers or feces from other dogs. Common parasites found in puppies include roundworms, hookworms, and whipworms. All of which are common sources of Great Dane puppy diarrhea.

Roundworms can be passed through the stool and can be easy to spot. To distinguish these in your dog's stool, look for organisms that resemble small spaghetti noodles. These are harmful to puppies since they deplete all necessary nutrients for development, ultimately stunting their growth. These parasites are passed by coming in contact with infected dog feces, earthworms, birds, and rodents.

Hookworms are blood-sucking parasites that invade dogs' small intestines. Some symptoms that indicate that your pup may be infected are severe diarrhea, pale lips, nose, and ears, and vomiting. It is also possible for these parasites to inhabit and live in a puppy's lungs. You can tell these are present if your dog starts to develop a consistent and unshakable cough.

Whipworms live in the large intestine and can be identified through microscopic eggs showing up in puppies' diarrhea. Dogs become infected by swallowing bacteria that are common from coming in contact with other dog's feces. Once a dog is infected, they can develop chronic diarrhea. At this point, veterinary intervention is required.

Vets are able to identify whipworms through medical tests. However, your dog should be tested multiple times since the parasites are tricky to catch. Because eggs are laid irregularly, tests will often come up negative even though whipworms are present.

Coccidia is a parasite found in feces and soil. Puppy's often contract it by coming into contact with their infected mother's feces, or by eating contaminated soil. Because puppy's immune systems take time to fully develop, they have minimal resistance to the organism. Great Danes between the ages of 4-12 weeks are usually the most affected. The most common symptom is severe diarrhea, however, vomiting and dehydration may also occur.

Giardia is an intestinal infection developed by ingesting infectious organisms through other dogs' feces. It is important to keep a close eye when your Great Dane is exposed to other playmates. You should also focus on keeping their environment clean from their own waste. Giardia parasites are known to cause diarrhea that is greasy, soft, or frothy and has a strong pungent odor and excessive mucus.

Chapter 8 - Diarrhea Sources and Treatment

If any parasites or worms are visible, you can purchase over-the-counter dewormers to help cope with the condition. These medications will generally treat all intestinal worms and are a must for Great Dane owners. If the problems persist, see a vet for assistance.

VIRAL INFECTIONS

Parvovirus, or parvo, is a viral disease that attacks the intestinal tract and white blood cells in dogs. It has been known to damage the heart muscle and results in cardiac problems. Your Great Dane puppy may be infected if they exhibit symptoms of lethargy, severe diarrhea, vomiting, or loss of appetite.

Canine distemper affects a dog's respiratory, nervous, and digestive systems, making it one of the most dangerous airborne diseases without a known cure. Common symptoms include red, watery eyes, discharge from the nose, lethargy, vomiting, and foul-smelling and bloody diarrhea.

Coronavirus infections also take place in the intestinal tract. Dogs contract Coronavirus by coming into contact with infected dogs' feces. Coronavirus is highly contagious. Dogs who have contracted this illness will exhibit uncontrollable diarrhea for several days along with depression, vomiting, loss of appetite, and mild fever. If diarrhea gets too severe to treat with home remedies, a trip to the vet may be necessary.

BACTERIAL INFECTION

Young Great Dane puppies are most at risk of contracting salmonella due to their underdeveloped immune system. In addition, dogs who are on antibiotics are more susceptible to salmonella. The antibiotics reduce the number of healthy bacteria to line their digestive tract, making them more vulnerable to the bacteria.

This infection can lead to inflammation of the stomach and intestine often resulting in diarrhea lasting for a few days. Other symptoms can include mild fever, shock, lethargy, vomiting, and weight loss. If you suspect your puppy to have salmonella, take him to the vet for stool analysis to determine for sure.

HOME REMEDIES FOR DIARRHEA

AVOID DEHYDRATION

To minimize the duration that your Great Dane puppy suffers from diarrhea, be sure that they are drinking plenty

Chapter 8 - Diarrhea Sources and Treatment

of water. It is important that these giant balls of love get enough fluids in their system since diarrhea can flush out vital liquids. Also, water helps to lubricate the gastrointestinal tract and remove any pathogens they may have ingested.

If your dog avoids their water bowl, try adding a bit of chicken broth to it. Voila! They will be lapping it up in no time

TRY A BLAND FOOD DIET

Feeding your Great Dane bland food like white rice, boiled chicken, and pureed pumpkin can help their digestive tract to function properly. By giving their digestive system a break from processing hard foods for a few days, their bowel irritation should disappear. Other bland food options that are safe for your pup include yogurt, boiled potatoes (without the skins), and cottage cheese.

Probiotics are also a wonderful addition to their food that can help soothe their gut. If diarrhea persists, some over-the-counter human medications like Pepcid can also be a good option. As always, check with your vet first before administering it.

FASTING

Sometimes episodes of diarrhea require your dog to start fasting. A 24-hour fast allows your dog's gut to rest and recover from the irritation in their stomachs.

Home remedies like rice water can be given to your dog while they are fasting. This is the creamy liquid that results from boiling white rice in water. However, it's important to use quality white rice when making rice water. Avoid brown rice as it contains too much fiber. This could speed up stool through the digestive tract, and create the opposite effect of what you want!

After your pup has fasted for a day or two, start him back on a bland diet of white rice cooked with extra water. From there, you can add baby food for added protein and flavor. Gradually move back to their normal food schedule.

WHEN TO SEE THE VETERINARIAN ABOUT DIARRHEA

It is normal for puppies and dogs to get upset stomachs now and then. The usual cases of diarrhea that you shouldn't worry about can be identified by the unmistakable smell and brown, chocolate pudding consistency. This is usually

Chapter 8 - Diarrhea Sources and Treatment

resolved through home remedies, rest, and staying hydrated. However, dogs who experience constant diarrhea for more than 2-3 consecutive days without solid stool should receive professional attention. Take them to a vet immediately for diagnosis and treatment.

It becomes something worth investigating further once dogs excrete black tarry stool or any stool with blood. Additional warning signs include:
- Consistent abdominal pain
- Groaning
- Vomiting
- Lethargy
- Bloating

Chronic diarrhea can be very dangerous for puppies and dogs. If it turns into an ongoing issue, it can deplete them of valuable nutrients needed for growth. Ultimately, it can also impair their immune system function. Seek veterinary assistance immediately if your pet is exhibiting these symptoms.

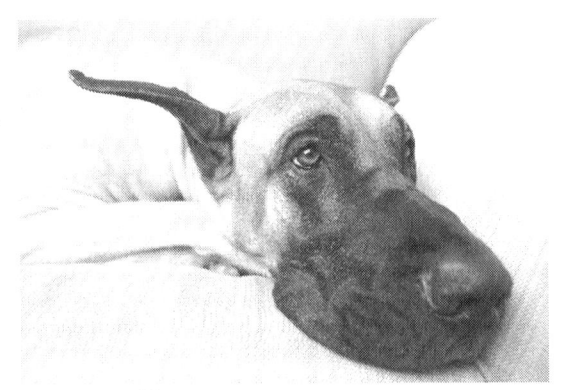

CHAPTER 9
ADDITIONAL CONSIDERATIONS

EXERCISE

General exercise through play is absolutely essential to the health and happiness of a Great Dane. It's also a fantastic way to release some of their puppy energy so that they're less likely to cause mischief around the house! However, because they grow so rapidly as puppies, you should avoid having them run with you on a leash until they are 18 months old.

This type of forced exercise could increase the risk of damage to their joints and lead to orthopedic issues later in life. These issues are often very expensive (thousands of dollars) and will also be very painful for your Great Dane.

Chapter 9 - Additional Considerations

This is not to say that they should not run at all, just that you shouldn't force them to run on a leash until they reach an appropriate age. Running for play in open areas off-leash is fine and recommended to help them healthy develop muscle tone.

While running on a leash is discouraged at a young age, leashed walks are completely safe due to being a much lower impact activity. For Great Danes under 6 months of age, keep your walks in the 5-15 minute range. If need be, you can take them on multiple walks per day. Once they reach 6-12 months in age, you can work up to one-hour walks while slowly increasing distance and time.

However, even at one year of age, many Great Danes will be content with a twenty-minute walk. So don't feel like you need to stretch out every outing to a full hour.

SOCIALIZATION

Great Danes are an incredibly friendly and social breed. However, it is still imperative that you expose them to a variety of people, places, and situations from a young age to properly socialize them. Socializing your Great Dane should be a major focal point from the time that you get them until

The Great Dane Puppy Handbook

they are at least 4 months in age. This is not to say that socialization ends at a certain point, just that it's important to expose them to a wide variety from a young age as this will greatly benefit them later on.

One of the best ways to socialize your Great Dane is to simply take them on walks! Compared to your home, walks expose your dog to a wide variety of new situations.

Hearing and seeing cars drive by, watching the mailman deliver mail, and seeing other people and dogs out walking are just a few of the things that your dog will experience on walks.

While it may seem like a small detail, introducing them to a wide variety of people is also important.

For example:
- Men
- Women
- Children
- People wearing hats, sunglasses, hoods, etc…
- People in uniform e.g. police, fireman, mailmen, etc…
- People of different races

Chapter 9 - Additional Considerations

In addition to a variety of people, you'll also want to continue mixing things up and expose them to additional settings and stimuli such as:

- Urban environments
- Different surfaces e.g. grass, sand, dirt, rocks
- Different animals e.g. cats, birds, squirrels, and other dogs
- Signs, strollers, bicycles, skateboards,

While already covered in the grooming section, you will want to spend plenty of time handling your Great Dane's face, ears, and paws to ensure that they are comfortable with these types of interaction.

PUPPY BITING

Great Danes may be known as the gentle giants of the dog world, but that doesn't mean some won't be prone to biting as puppies. Puppies use their mouths to play and explore the world, so don't take it as a sign that you have an "aggressive" Great Dane if you find them nipping. Unfortunately, biting is also one of the ways that they learned how to play with their littermates from a young age, so it will take time to teach them that biting and nipping at their human family is inappropriate.

In addition to play and exploration, your puppy may also bite more during teething. Many find it soothing to their aching gums to bite into something soft - which unfortunately can often be your finger or arm! While this can be painful, the good news is that it is something that you can train them out of. There are several methods of training your puppy to stop biting, all of which involve interrupting the behavior in some fashion.

Keep in mind that you can easily use several of the methods described below at a time to really drive the message home. However, the key will be consistent feedback to the behavior. Don't expect results overnight. It takes time to break habits and for a puppy to grow to a maturity level where it can overcome instinctual behaviors. Be patient, and keep at it!

THE SHARP CRY METHOD

When littermate puppies are playing, and one of them goes too far and hurts another, the injured pup will yelp, hide the affected body part, and turn away. Playtime ends while the injured puppy recovers. This method involves mimicking the response of an injured playmate to teach your dog that biting hurts.

Chapter 9 - Additional Considerations

1. **Get Bitten:** When your dog bites, even if it's soft or doesn't hurt, you need to respond. As your puppy grows into an adult Great Dane, he or she may struggle to understand their newfound strength. Avoid problems down the road by discouraging all biting now.
2. **Yelp:** Make a loud, sharp, high pitched yelp or squeal. You want to mimic the sound of a puppy as well as you can.
3. **Hide the Affected Body Part:** If you were bitten, for example, on your hand, you would pull your hand close to you and turn away from your dog. Place your body between you and where you were bitten.
4. **Walk Away:** Playtime is now over. Your Great Dane needs to learn that if they want to keep playing, they need to play nice. Walk away and wait some time before engaging with the dog again. Some owner's instead of walking away will place the dog in a kennel or cage as a time out to show the dog that they are the ones in control.
5. **Be Consistent**: Keep this up every time your puppy bites, and eventually, they'll associate biting with causing harm and ending playtime. The negative association will prevent them from biting in the future.

THE DISTRACTION METHOD

Using distraction to direct your dog's attention away from biting people and towards more acceptable alternatives, such as chew toys can be a great way to encourage better behaviors.

1. **Get Bitten:** Once again, you need to respond every time your dog bites you. Consistency is key.
2. **Pull Away the Bitten Body Part:** You need to immediately pull away whenever your dog bites. The more immediate, the stronger the dog will build the association between the behavior and the response.
3. **Immediately Offer a Chew Toy:** You'll probably want to keep a toy, a bone, or a rope in hand while playing with your dog. That way, when he or she bites, you can immediately offer the alternative.
4. **Reward Successful Play Sessions:** When you get through an entire play session with no biting incidents, offer a preferred treat as a reward.

THE LEADER OF THE PACK METHOD

Dogs are pack animals with distinct leadership hierarchies. You need to ensure that your dog respects you as the pack leader. This distinction comes with dedicated training and demanding strict obedience.

Chapter 9 - Additional Considerations

1. **Train Your Dog:** Teach your dog some basic tricks like "sit" and "stay." Teaching these basic maneuvers and rewarding them with treats will establish you as the provider of food and the one in charge.
2. **House Train:** House training is similar to training a dog not to bite in that it's training a dog not to do something more so than how to do something. House training will allow you to build negative associations with a firm tone of voice and words like "no" or "bad dog."
3. **Get Bitten:** If you've established yourself as the alpha and your dog bites you anyway, you cannot take it lying down. Even a small nibble may be a way of testing the limits of your dominance. Don't give an inch. If your dog tries to bite, shout "No!" in a firm tone of voice.
4. **Reward Successful Play Sessions:** When you get through a play session with no biting incidents, offer a treat as a reward. Positive reinforcement will strengthen your relationship and give your dog greater respect for your leadership.

Pick A Training Approach

While there are many important aspects to caring for a Great Dane, providing them with proper training may be one of the most important. As one of the world's largest dogs, they very well may be larger and stronger than you once they are full grown. Regardless of whether you get your Great Dane as a puppy or adult, training should be one of your top priorities. A well-trained Great Dane is guaranteed to lead a safer, happier, and more fulfilling life than one who is untrained.

Because the process for obedience training deserves its own book, it will not be covered here. Instead, what will be covered is guiding you through the training options available. Use this information to make an informed decision on how you will train your Great Dane when the time comes.

Private Training

While private training is the most expensive option, it often leads to the fastest results. Working 1-on-1 with an instructor allows for the most direct guidance and greatest attention to detail to your Great Dane. They also have the freedom to better tailor the training to the specific needs of the dog and can adapt or make changes when necessary.

Chapter 9 - Additional Considerations

GROUP TRAINING

Group training classes are typically set up such that 1-2 trainers lead of group of owners and dogs. Class sizes are usually capped to prevent there from being too many dogs for the trainers to pay attention to. They sometimes result in slower results due to the decrease in direct attention, but this will be somewhat dependent on your skills as a trainer and your dog's aptitude. Most trainers will help as much as they can, however, they will still have other dogs and owners in the class to assist as well.

In addition to being cheaper than private training, group classes do have the added benefit of forcing your Great Dane to learn new skills in the presence of distractions i.e. other dogs. Exhibiting perfect behavior while no distractions are present is helpful, but the true test of a dog's training is how they perform when conditions are not perfect. If your Great Dane can perfectly execute basic commands such as sit, down, or come in the presence of a dozen other dogs, then chances are that they will be able to do so almost anywhere.

SELF-LED TRAINING

Last but not least, is the self-led training approach. While its comparatively cheaper cost is certainly nice, its flexibility may be the largest benefit. Whether you've purchased access to an online course, watched YouTube videos, or learned from other free resources, you have the option of training your Great Dane when and where it's convenient for you.

Now, this convenience can also act as a negative. You will need to have the self-discipline to ensure that you train with your Great Dane on a regularly scheduled basis. Repetition is key, so taking a month off between training will not lead to the best results. If sticking to a schedule is not your strong suit, you may want to consider looking into group or private training sessions.

POTTY TRAINING

While obedience training is not covered, no Great Dane puppy book could be considered complete without a chapter on potty training! While potty training is typically not a tough process for Great Danes, there are common mistakes made by owners that make it more difficult.

One such common mistake is the use of pee pads. Pee pads quite literally encourage your dog to relieve themselves indoors. Because this is the opposite of our ultimate goal,

Chapter 9 - Additional Considerations

their use should be avoided at all costs. So, spare your dog the confusion and skip the pee pads.

The key for easy potty training ultimately boils down to creating a schedule for your dog. That schedule begins with deciding when you will feed your Great Dane. Consistently feeding your dog the same number of meals is important because these large boluses of food are one of the main drivers of bowel movements.

If you're switching from three small meals one day, to one giant meal the next day, their digestive system will literally be kept guessing. This is bad news for you when you're trying to leverage a well-timed digestive process for your own means with potty training. By consistently feeding them the same number of meals each day, you can expect that they will need to use the bathroom within 30 minutes after finishing each meal.

In addition to the meal frequency, the relative timing of meals is also important to keep as steady as possible. For example, if you're feeding your dog two meals per day, you might want to go with 8 am and 5 pm. Try to feed them their meals at these exact times each day. A few minutes in either direction is not an issue, you just want to avoid moving a mealtime by a couple of hours. Also, don't feel like you have to stick to eight and five as I used in the example. Pick mealtimes that are reasonable for your daily schedule and that you know you can stick to.

In addition to making it a habit to take your Great Dane to the bathroom after meals, there are a few other key times that you should put on your schedule as well. Some of these may also come up in an ad hoc sense but should give you an idea of when you can expect your dog to need to relieve themselves.

Remember – the key is to take advantage of these situations and use them as positive reinforcement for going to the bathroom in the appropriate area.

- **Waking up:** Regardless of whether or not your dog used the bathroom overnight, the first thing that you should do with them in the morning is to take them outside to relieve themselves. Not only is this typically one of the longest breaks between going, but their bodies have had a chance to process much of the food and water from the previous day. Needless to say – your dog will be ready to go!

Chapter 9 - Additional Considerations

- **Before bed:** Much like how you take them out immediately after waking up, you should also allow them to relieve themselves just prior to bedtime. Once again, the night is usually one of their longest stretches, so you want to give them the chance to go before being tucked in for the night.
- **After naps:** Great Danes of all ages are fantastic nappers! However, especially during their younger years, there's a good chance that they'll need to use the bathroom after a nap. After relaxing and allowing their bodies to process food and water, it shouldn't be a surprise that it's potty time again!
- **Play and training:** After a good play or training session, it's quite typical that your dog will need to relieve themselves. Sometimes this may even happen halfway through a play session, so keep a close eye on them if this is occurring indoors!
- **Excitement:** Nothing stirs up a bowel movement like some good ole fashioned excitement! Whether it's meeting a new friend, getting a new toy, etc.. watch out for some unplanned potty breaks around these exciting events.

If you've taken the steps previously mentioned then you will definitely have a great start on anticipating your dog's bathroom needs. However, there will still be unexpected times that come up when your Great Dane needs to go potty. This is absolutely normal and to be expected, your job is to simply ensure that it doesn't happen inside your home!

While every dog is different and will have their own telltale signs, here a few signals that might indicate that your dog needs to go to the bathroom.

- Spinning in circles
- Sniffing around
- Whining or showing other signs of discomfort
- Sniffing or licking their groin or rear
- Returning to the area where a previous accident occurred
- Pawing or whining at the door or exit typically used to go outside

If you notice that your Great Dane is showing any of these signs, make sure to quickly take them outside to use the bathroom. While you're going to make more trips outside than are actually necessary, it's far better than having to clean up the mess inside! It shouldn't take too long until you're able to identify your dog's specific signals that they need to use the bathroom.

Chapter 9 - Additional Considerations

Alright, now that we've covered all of the possible missteps that can thwart potty training, let's talk about the specifics of the actual training portion.

Before starting, you'll want to take care of a few final decisions:

- **Pick the place** that your dog will relieve themselves. Even if you have a large yard or open area, pick a set area to reinforce the process for your dog in these early days.
- **Choose which command** you will use to associate with your dog relieving themselves. Common choices are "go potty", "outside", "pee", etc... It doesn't matter what you pick, just that you're consistent with it.
- **Select the exit door** that will be used during potty training and stick to it exclusively throughout the process. This helps to reinforce the process for your dog by removing as many variables as possible.

Alright, now that you've got these final items buttoned-up, let's walk through the steps for potty training.

These steps will already assume that you're taking your dog out to go potty based on a normal schedule, or other sign that leads you to believe that they need to go to the bathroom.

1. Place your dog on their leash
2. Walk them to the designated exit door
3. Guide them to the predetermined bathroom area
4. Keeping them on-leash, wait for them to relieve themselves
5. As soon as they start to pee or poop, clearly say your potty word/phrase e.g. "go potty"
6. After they finish relieving themselves, celebrate like you just won the lottery!

While this may seem incredibly simple, I can assure you that it is effective!

First, because you have prevented all of the common missteps that most make with potty training, you're almost guaranteed that your dog will need to go to the bathroom when you take them out. With this type of diligence, you've also done a great job of preventing them from going in the wrong place. Which is more than half of the battle!

Chapter 9 - Additional Considerations

Secondly, and I can't understate its importance here – is the need to truly celebrate your dog's successful potty breaks. Great Danes love attention and affection from their humans, so don't short change them here. By associating going potty in the right place as a very positive event, you're incenting them to want to do it right every time.

While some people like to start this process by stating the potty word, my preference is to time it more closely to the actual act of your dog relieving themselves. This makes it much clearer that "go potty" is the act of going to the bathroom, and not something else.

This is also why I like to keep the dog on the leash during this process.

- It prevents them from taking a detour and deciding to pee/poop in the wrong spot along the way
- It keeps you on the hook to supervise the process and not get distracted playing with your phone!
- It allows you to continue going to a consistent spot area for bathroom breaks and limits wandering
- If your dog doesn't get used to going to the bathroom on-leash early, it's going to be much harder to teach it later

Even while following these careful steps, there are bound to be accidents. However, as long as you're putting in your own best effort they should be few and far between. When they do happen, don't force your dog's face into it or yell and scream at them.

Great Danes are very sensitive and will be able to tell that you're upset with them without all of that commotion. Furthermore, if you're not catching them in the act of it, they would have no idea what they're even in trouble for.

In the event that you do catch them in the act, immediately initiate the normal potty training process. This gives them a chance to complete relieving themselves in the right place, where you can provide the proper positive reinforcement.

Registration Requirements

Depending on where you live, you may be required to register your dog with the local authorities. Because these regulations vary wildly and change frequently, I'm not able to create an exhaustive list here. Just know that you should perform your own due diligence to stay in compliance and avoid potential fines.

Chapter 9 - Additional Considerations

Some municipalities only look for certification from a veterinarian that the animal is in good health, whereas others require actual registration for tracking purposes. While there are often costs associated with registering your Great Dane, they are always less than the cost of a fine so it's best to stay in compliance.

Last but not least, make sure to also keep any required registration tags attached to your Great Dane's collar at all times. These are useful not just for proof of registration, but also for locating the owners of lost dogs.

CHAPTER 10
CLOSING THOUGHTS

While taking action on each of the steps detailed in this book will put you well ahead of the curve compared to other new owners, it is not an exhaustive list. Unexpected events are bound to occur, and it will be your responsibility as the owner to watch out for them. When these circumstances do occur, make sure to take action on them by contacting your veterinarian for advice.

Small grooming tasks such as brushing, nail trimming, and ear cleaning may seem mundane, but performing them on a regular basis will keep you in tune with any changes in your Great Dane. The faster that diseases and other ailments are identified, the faster that they can be professionally treated.

Chapter 10 - Closing Thoughts

Bringing home a Great Dane puppy is clearly no small undertaking, but doing so usually ends in the addition of a new best friend. Dogs may be referred to as "man's best friend" but Great Danes take this saying to an entirely new level! Keep in mind that every puppy will still have their bad days, but these are short-lived in comparison to the overall time that you will spend together.

Great Danes grow at such an incredible pace throughout their first year that you will want to make sure to savor each and every moment with them. Before you know it, their cute wrinkly puppy days will be long behind them and they will have transformed into the wonderful, giant, and sometimes goofy dogs that they are. Make sure to document these times with photographs and videos so that you will have them available to reminisce many years later. There is no doubt that owning and caring for a Great Dane is a journey, but it's one well worth enjoying!

About the Author

Zach Reed is a lifelong Great Dane fan and advocate for the breed. In addition to owning and caring for Great Danes, he has helped thousands of other people care for their dogs. To further improve the public knowledge about caring for Great Danes, Zach founded GreatDaneCare.com as a free resource for owners around the world.

Zach takes a no-nonsense approach to his writing that makes use of his own first-hand knowledge, as well as from consulting with breeders and veterinarians around the United States. Zach lives in Colorado with his family and enjoys spending time in the beautiful outdoors. He looks forward to continuing to produce Great Dane-related resources to help others for many years to come.

To learn more about Great Danes or to contact Zach, you can do so at https://greatdanecare.com.

Printed in Great Britain
by Amazon